# META CUBE
# Sacred Geometry Notebook

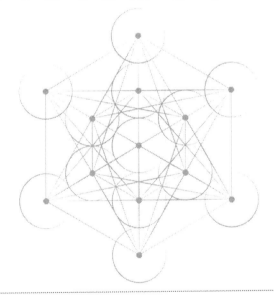

This Notebook Belongs To:

E-mail:

Phone:

# GOALS:

☐

☐

☐

☐

☐

☐

☐

☐

☐

☐

## Accomplishments:

○ _____

○ _____

○ _____

○ _____

○ _____

○ _____

○ _____

○ _____

○ _____

○ _____

| Habit Tracker | 1 | 2 | 3 | 4 | 5 | 6 | 7 | 8 | 9 | 10 |
|---|---|---|---|---|---|---|---|---|---|---|
|  |  |  |  |  |  |  |  |  |  |  |
|  |  |  |  |  |  |  |  |  |  |  |
|  |  |  |  |  |  |  |  |  |  |  |
|  |  |  |  |  |  |  |  |  |  |  |
|  |  |  |  |  |  |  |  |  |  |  |

## Appointments & Special Dates:

# https://Inspirational Wares.com

  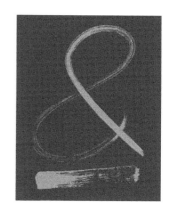

For more amazing journals and adult coloring books visit:
*Amazon.com*
*CreateSpace.com*
*InspirationalWares.com*

She Believed She Could
So She Did
Adult Coloring Book

The Adult Coloring Book
for Coffee Lovers

Yoga – An Adult Coloring Book

The Ultimate Adult Coloring
Book for Men

Made in the USA
San Bernardino, CA
30 November 2017